THEMATIC UNIT
Families

Written by Liz Rothlein, Ed. D.

Teacher Created Materials, Inc.
6421 Industry Way
Westminster, CA 92683
www.teachercreated.com
©1997 Teacher Created Materials, Inc.
Reprinted, 2001
Made in U.S.A.
ISBN-1-57690-110-6

Illustrated by
Barbara Lorseydi

Edited by
Barbara M. Wally, M.S.

Cover Art by
Sue Fullam

Table of Contents

Introduction

Families contains a captivating whole language thematic unit. Its 80 pages are filled with a wide variety of lesson ideas and reproducible pages designed for use with children at the early childhood level. At its core are two high quality children's literature selections, *All Kinds of Families* and *Poinsettia and Her Family*. Activities which set the stage for reading, encourage the enjoyment of the book, and extend the concepts gained are included for each of these featured books. In addition, the theme is connected to the curriculum with activities in language arts (including language experience and writing suggestions), math, science, art, life skills, and music and movement. Many of the activities encourage cooperative learning. Suggestions and patterns for bulletin boards, learning center activities, and directions for student-created Big Books are time savers for busy teachers. Additionally, directions are given for a culminating activity, which allows the children to synthesize their knowledge by creating products that can be shared beyond the classroom. This thematic unit includes the following:

☐ **literature selections**—summaries of two children's books with related lessons (complete with reproducible pages) that cross the curriculum

☐ **planning guides**—suggestions for sequencing lessons each day of the unit

☐ **language experience and writing ideas**—suggestions for activities across the curriculum

☐ **bulletin board ideas**—suggestions and plans for student-created and/or interactive bulletin boards

☐ **curriculum connections**—suggestions for activities in language arts, math, science, art, music, social studies' and life skills like physical education and cooking

☐ **group projects**—suggestions for projects to foster cooperative learning

☐ **a culminating activity**—suggestions for a celebration which requires students to synthesize their learning in an activity to be shared with others

☐ **a bibliography**—suggestions for additional literature and nonfiction books on the theme

To keep this valuable resource intact so it can be used year after year, you may wish to punch holes in the pages and store them in a three-ring binder.

Introduction *(cont.)*

Why the Balanced Approach?

The strength of a whole language approach involves children using all modes of communication—reading, writing, listening, observing, illustrating, and speaking. Communication skills are integrated into lessons which emphasize the whole of language. Balancing this approach is our knowledge that every whole—including individual words—is composed of parts, and directed study of those parts can help a student to master the whole. Experience and research tell us that regular attention to phonics, other word attack skills, spelling, etc., develops reading mastery, thereby completing the unity of the whole language experience. The child is thus led to read, write, spell, speak, listen, and think in response to a literature experience introduced by the teacher. In these ways language skills grow steadily, stimulated by direct practice, involvement, and interest in the topic at hand.

Why Thematic Planning?

One useful tool for implementing a balanced language program is thematic planning. By choosing a theme with corresponding literature selections for a unit of study, a teacher can plan activities throughout the day that lead to cohesive, in-depth study of the topic. Students practice and apply their skills in meaningful contexts. Consequently, they tend to learn and retain more. Both teachers and students are freed from a day that is broken into unrelated segments of isolated drill and practice.

Why Cooperative Learning?

In addition to academic skills and content, students need to learn social skills. No longer can this area of development be taken for granted. Students must learn to work cooperatively in groups in order to function well in modern society. Group activities should be a regular part of school life, and teachers should consciously include social objectives as well as academic objectives in their planning. The teacher should clarify and monitor the qualities of good group interaction just as he/she would clarify and monitor the academic goals of a project.

Why Big Books?

An excellent cooperative, balanced language activity is the production of Big Books. Groups of students, or the whole class, can apply their language skills, content knowledge, and creativity to produce a Big Book that can become a part of the classroom library to be read and reread. These books make excellent culminating projects for sharing beyond the classroom with parents, librarians, visitors, and other classes. Big Books can be produced in many ways, and this thematic unit book includes directions for at least one method you may choose.

All Kinds of Families

by Norma Simon

Summary

This book explores in words and pictures what a family is and how families vary in makeup and lifestyles. It acknowledges that families are not always composed in the traditional way of two parents and children. It also stresses the supportive function of the family and the child's joyous place in the center of his or her world. It is a very realistic book that deals with happy times as well as sad times.

The outline below is a suggested plan for using the various activities that are presented in this unit. You should adapt these ideas to fit your classroom situations.

Sample Plan

Day 1

- Introduce the book *All Kinds of Families*. See Setting the Stage, activity 5, page 6.
- Read approximately the first half of the book.
- Discuss family sizes, Enjoying the Book, activity 2, page 6.
- Practice writing family words, pages 42 and 43.
- Select a Music and Movement activity, pages 64–66.

Day 2

- Read the last half of the book.
- Review groups and sizes; complete the activity on page 13.
- Do the family name activity, page 11.
- Complete the Families Grow and Change activity, page 14.
- Introduce picture journals, page 41.
- Select a family finger play, page 48.
- Send home copies of page 27, My Family Tree.

Day 3

- Reread and review the book
- Create pop-up family portraits, page 59.
- Discuss visiting relatives and assign page 10.
- Play "I Packed My Suitcase," Enjoying the Book, activity 5, page 7.
- Assign a picture journal topic, page 41.
- Select a Music and Movement activity, pages 64–66.
- Complete the House Dot-to-Dot, page 19.

Day 4

- Discuss ways that families help each other and complete page 12.
- Do a graphing activity, page 57.
- Complete Morning to Night, page 21.
- Play Relative Concentration, page 23.
- Make Family Puppets, page 58.
- Assign a picture journal topic, page 41.
- Select a Music and Movement activity, pages 64–66.

Day 5

- Complete activity 2 on page 7, Our Classroom Family.
- Play "Mother, May I?" page 66.
- Discuss family celebrations and complete the activity on page 53.
- Create pop-up cards or letters to family members, activity 6, page 7.
- Begin making the All About My Family book, pages 15–18.
- Match families and houses, page 22.

Day 6

- Review family words and assign Who Am I? page 49.
- Create an acrostic with the word "family," page 41.
- Continue All About My Family books.
- Begin Quilting Time, page 9.

Day 7

- Discuss similarities and differences among families and assign pages 46 and 47.
- Continue quilt project.
- Match children and families, page 25.
- Make family puzzles, page 63.
- Select a family finger play, page 48.
- Assign a picture journal topic, page 41.
- Complete In All Kinds of Weather, page 20.

Overview of Activities

Setting the Stage

1. Prepare and display one of the bulletin boards from page 74.

2. Send the letter on page 75 to all parents, explaining the unit and soliciting their help in fostering concepts presented in this unit.

3. Using the bibliography on page 80, collect other books related to families. Then designate a special area in the classroom in which to display these books. Provide seating for children to use when they visit this library corner. As the unit progresses, encourage the children to contribute books they have created about their families to the collection.

4. Create one or more of the learning activity centers described on page 72.

5. Gather the children together and show them the book, *All Kinds of Families*. Read the title and show them the cover illustration. Ask the children what the title *All Kinds of Families* means to them. Lead them into discussing their family members and relatives, all the people they think make up their families.

6. Ask the children to name some family members. As they do so, record the relative words on chart paper or on the chalkboard to make a word bank. Group words by the relationship. There will be different names for the same relationship—one child's grandma is another's grammy or nana.

7. Make copies of pages 42 and 43. Have the children add features to the faces and practice tracing the words for family members. Older or more advanced children may copy the words on the lines provided.

Enjoying the Book

1. Over the period of several days, read *All Kinds of Families* to the children. There is a lot to absorb in this book, and the illustrations are interesting. Make sure the children are seated close around you so they can enjoy and learn from the illustrations. Pause frequently to ask comprehension questions and elicit personal responses to the concepts as they are presented. After each reading session, make sure the book is available for the children to browse through. Some questions to ask are What is a family? Who makes up your family? When do families get together? What are some things families do when they get together? Do all members of a family live together in the same place? Explain. What is an aunt? an uncle? a cousin? a niece? a nephew? a grandparent? What makes a family special?

2. Families, like people, come in many different shapes and sizes. As a group, list all the different kinds of families mentioned in this book. For example, families with two parents, families with one parent, families with grown children, etc. Use the figures on pages 76 and 77 and a flannel board to illustrate the different groupings. Ask the children to think of any other different kinds of families that were not mentioned in the book. Stress that all the groups are families.

3. Ask the children how many people are in their families as you record numbers on the chalkboard. Determine which is the biggest family, which is the smallest family, and which family is middle-sized. Discuss ages and record them in the same manner.

4. Relatives often go to visit each other. Ask the children to share their visits with relatives. Where did they go? Who did they see? Post a large map on the bulletin board. Pin a square of colored construction paper over your city, and use yarn or string to connect the places children have visited.

6

Overview of Activities *(cont.)*

Enjoying the Book *(cont.)*

5. Discuss what you need to take if you stay overnight. Ask the children to share what they would take along on an overnight trip by drawing the items in the suitcase, page 10. To extend this activity, play I Packed My Suitcase, page 65.

6. Families like to tell each other where they are and what they are doing by sending each other letters, postcards, and birthday cards. Reread these pages to the children. Ask them if they have received mail from a family member. Was it a special occasion? When do we send cards and/or letters to people? Have the children make pop-up greeting card, page 59, to send to someone in their families. Ask the parents to provide the address and appropriate postage, and mail the completed cards. As an alternative, give each child a copy of the stationery on page 78 to take home. Ask parents to help their children write a letter to a family member. To extend this activity, mark the destination of each card or letter on a map. After a week or more, ask the children if they have received responses and record them on the map.

7. Family members help each other and work together to get things done. Ask the children to think of ways in which they can help their families and to complete page 12. Tell the children that they may draw something they already do or something that they can begin doing. Post the completed drawings on a bulletin board. Allow time to discuss the various ways in which the children are going to help their families.

8. Members of a family often have the same last name. Have the children complete the activity on page 11. Display the finished pictures in ABC order. To extend the activity, ask the children to count how many there are of each letter. Are there children with the same last name?

9. Follow the directions on page 9 to create a class quilt. Display the quilt in the classroom, library, or on a hallway wall.

10. Make pop-up family portraits, page 59. Use photographs or the children's art. In addition, discuss things they like to do with different family members/relatives. Display the family portraits on the bulletin board.

Extending the Book

1. Provide the children with an assortment of magazines or ask them to bring in magazine pictures of different kinds of families doing things together. Make a collage of these pictures and title it "All Shapes, All Sizes." Allow time to discuss the similarities and differences among the pictures.

2. Families are made up of individuals. Ask the children to think about ways in which their class is like a family. Read the following statements and ask the children if they are true for both the class and their families. We play together. We care about each other's feelings. We sometimes disagree with each other. We sometimes have to do things we don't want to do. We have lots of different people.

   Make a copy of page 24 for each child. Ask the child to paste a recent photo of himself or herself in the frame. If no photo is available, have the child draw a self-portrait in the frame. Assist the in answering the statements about themselves. Bind the completed pages into a Big Book with the title "Our Classroom Family." Display the book in the reading corner. If a camera and film are available, expand on the theme, adding pictures of the children at work and play in the classroom.

Overview of Activities *(cont.)*

Extending the Book *(cont.)*

3. Ask the parents to supply a snapshot-size family photo, or have the children draw family pictures the size of a snapshot. Make copies of page 15 on construction paper. Have the children write their names in the blanks and cut out their patterns. Place each child's photo or picture on the house where the front door would be and trace around it. Cut inside the right side and top of the traced line and fold on the left side of the line to create a door. Tape the photo or picture behind the door. Have the children color and decorate their houses.

   Make copies of pages 16–18 for each child. Ask them to complete the pages by drawing the members of their families. If desired, change the words to create additional pages, like "My family at work," "My family at play," "My grandparents," etc.

   When the pages are complete, staple or bind the books with yarn. Invite the children to share their books and their families with the class.

4. Ask the children to decide on a holiday or other special time, like a birthday, that their families celebrate. Have them complete the activity on page 53, drawing themselves and adding a food or decoration to show what is being celebrated.

5. Families grow and change. Although new families are formed, they are still part of the older families. Discuss how new families are formed when people marry and that the new family is part of both the mother's family and the father's family. Help the children complete and illustrate the Venn diagram on page 26.

6. Send copies of page 27 home. Ask parents to assist their children in completing family trees. Allow children to share their family trees as you ask specific questions such as: How many grandparents do you have altogether? How many parents do you have? Display the family trees on a bulletin board. Encourage the children to compare and contrast their family trees.

7. Make two copies of page 23. Use markers, crayons, or colored pencils to color the pictures. Mount the pages on poster board or tagboard, laminate them, and cut them apart. Store the completed picture cards in envelopes. Use the cards for one or more of the following activities.

   Matching The child arranges the cards from one envelope faceup on the table. He or she then finds the matching card from the second envelope and places it beside the first card.

   Generations Ask the child to identify the pairs in one set of the cards, e.g., grandmother and grandfather. Challenge older or more advanced children to arrange the sets in generational order.

   Concentration The cards may also be used to play a concentration game for one or two players. Turn all the cards facedown on a table. The child turns over two of the cards. If they match, he or she holds them. If they do not match, the cards are returned to the table, facedown. Continue until all the matches have been made.

8. Make a copy of page 19 for each child. Teach or review the numbers 1–9. Have the children connect the dots to complete the pattern.

   Variation: To make lacing cards, glue copies of page 19 to poster board or other heavy paper (the inside of cereal boxes works well). Laminate the pages if desired. Cut around the pattern, leaving a $1/2$-inch (1.25 cm) border. Punch a hole at each number. Provide shoelaces, ribbon, or yarn for lacing. Wrap the ends of yarn or ribbon with tape, or dip them in colorless nail polish to prevent fraying.

8

Quilting Time

Show the children the illustration of family members sewing a quilt together in *All Kinds of Families*. If possible, show them a real patchwork quilt, pointing out the different squares. Children may have quilts at home they can bring to share.

Tell the children that they will be working together to make a class quilt. You may wish to read and/or display some of the following books before you make the quilt.

Mrs. Noah's Patchwork Quilt by Janet Bolton. (Andrews, 1995)

The Patchwork Quilt by Valerie Flournoy. (Dial Books, 1985)

The Canada Geese Quilt by Natalie Kinsey. (Dell, 1992)

Sam Johnson and the Blue Ribbon Quilt by Lisa C. Ernst. (Lothrop, Lee and Shepard, 1983)

The Keeping Quilt by Patricia Polacco. (Simon and Schuster, 1988)

The Quilt by Ann Jonas. (Greenwillow, 1984)

The Quilt Story by Tony Johnston. (Putnam, 1992)

The Josefina Story Quilt by Eleanor Coerr. (HarperCollins, 1989)

Cemetery Quilt by Kent and Alice Ross. (Houghton, 1995)

Materials: construction paper in assorted colors, cut in 8 inch (20 cm) squares, pencils and/or crayons or markers

Directions: Ask the children to select a square and draw a picture that represents their families on their squares. Some examples are a pet, something they enjoy doing with their families, their homes, etc. After they have completed their squares, fit them together on the bulletin board to resemble a quilt. Put a one inch (2.54 cm) border of construction paper around the entire quilt. Title the bulletin board "Our Class Is a Family."

Variations

1. Have the children cut illustrations from magazines and paste them to their squares.

2. Punch holes at ½-inch (1.25 cm) intervals around each square. Provide yarn, string, or other lacing material. When the children complete their squares, have them work in pairs to "sew" their quilt blocks together by aligning the holes and lacing. Next, have each pair work with another pair to join their squares. Continue until the quilt is assembled.

3. Show some samples of traditional quilt block patterns. Provide a variety of geometric shapes (rectangles, squares, triangles) cut from colored construction paper, patterned gift wrap, or wallpaper sample books. Ask children to arrange the shapes on the larger square to create a quilt block. When they have decided on a pattern, have them paste the shapes to the block.

4. Use squares of felt in place of construction paper. The children may draw or paste on their squares. For this variation you may wish to ask parents to supply scraps of fabric that are meaningful to the children. Felt squares may be sewed together using yarn and a large, blunt yarn needle or punched and laced as above.

Name _____

Going Visiting

Directions: Pretend you are going to stay overnight with a relative. Draw all the things you would take along with you in the suitcase below. Put a circle around the item you think is most important to take along.

Name _____

Every Family Has a Name

Last names are family names. Many people in a family share the same last name. Write the first letter of your last name in the box below, and then draw yourself sitting on the letter. **Note:** Older or more advanced children can draw or paste pictures of things that begin with the same letter in the box.

Name _____

Helping Hand

Directions: On the hand draw a picture of something that you can do to help your family, and then cut out the hand.

Name _____

All Sizes, All Shapes

Families come in all sizes. Some are big, some are middle-sized, and some are small. Below are some pictures of different-sized families. Do the following:

Draw a circle around the biggest family.

Draw a square around the smallest family.

Name _____

Families Grow and Change

Directions: Color the pictures below. Cut out the pictures and paste them on another piece of paper to show how the family grows and changes.

All About My Family

Directions: See Extending the Book, activity 3, page 8, for directions.

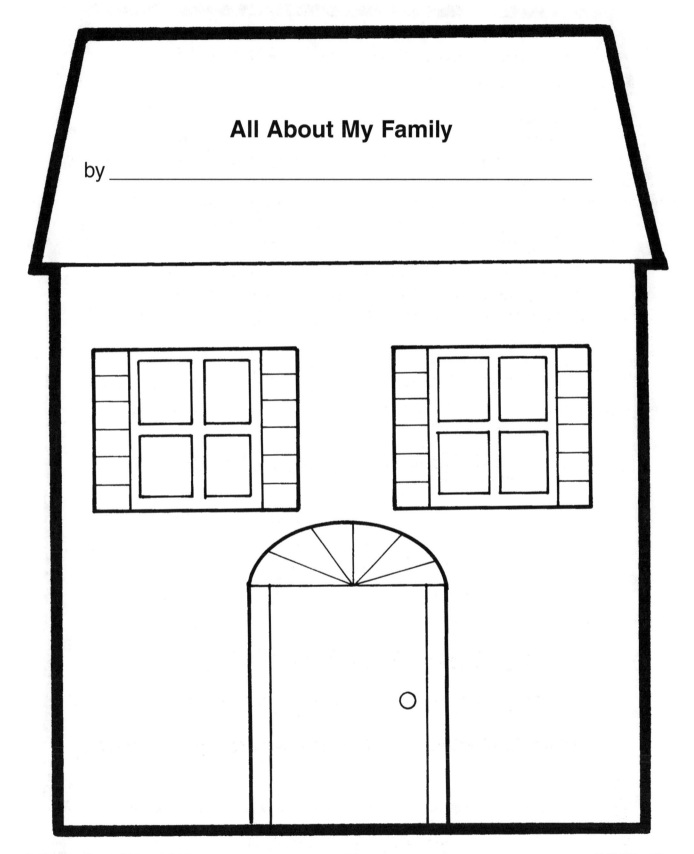

All About My Family

by _____

All About My Family *(cont.)*

This is my family. There are_____people in my family.

All About My Family *(cont.)*

I like to_____with my father.

I like to_____with my mother.

This is my mother.

This is my father.

All About My Family *(cont.)*

I have_____sisters and_____ brothers.

We like to_____together.

Name _____

House Dot-to-Dot

Directions: Connect the dots to finish the picture. Color the picture and add people to live in the house.

Name _____

In All Kinds of Weather

Directions: Draw a picture of what you like to do with your family during the following weather conditions.

When it is warm and sunny, I like to _____with my family.

When it is raining, I like to _____with my family.

When it is cold and snowy, I like to _____with my family.

When it is windy, I like to _____with my family.

Name _____

Morning to Night

Directions: Here are some things that members of families do each day. Cut apart the pictures below and paste them in the boxes in the order in which you do them each day. Color each picture.

Name _____

All Kinds of Houses

Directions: Each of the families below lives in one of the houses. Draw a line from each family to its house. Write the family number on the line. Color the families and the houses. Hint: There is one window for each family member.

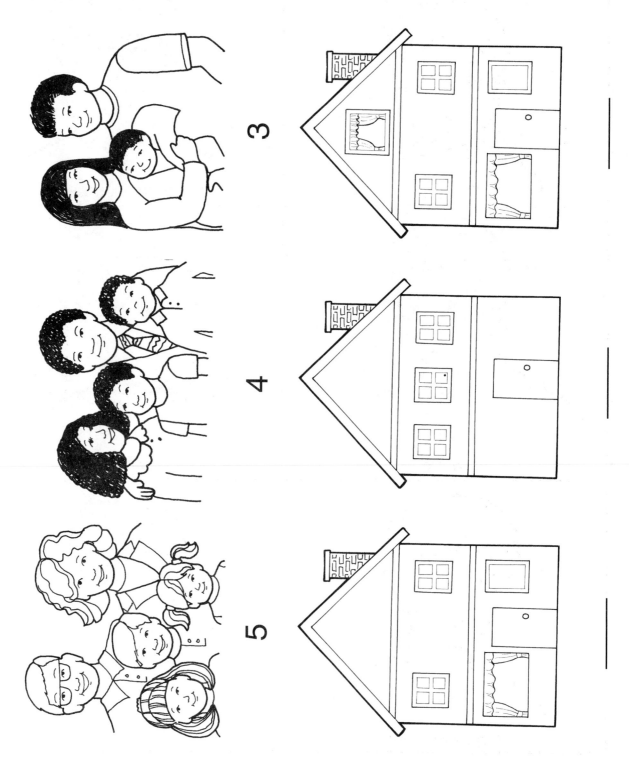

Relative Concentration

Directions: See Extending the Book, activity 7, page 8.

Our Classroom Family

All About _____

(name)

I was born on _____ _____, _____.

                      (month)   (day)   (year)

I was born in_____.

(place)

I am_____inches (cm) tall.

I weigh_____pounds (kg).

My favorite color is_____.

My favorite foods are_____.

My favorite book/story is_____.

The thing I like most about school is

_____.

Name _____

Belonging

Can you tell which children belong to which parents? Color matching patterns the the same color.

How Families Grow

A Venn diagram shows what two or more groups have in common. Use markers or colored pencils to shade one circle pink and the other blue. What color is the overlapping area? Add pictures of the people named on this diagram to see how new families are formed and how the members of your family are related.

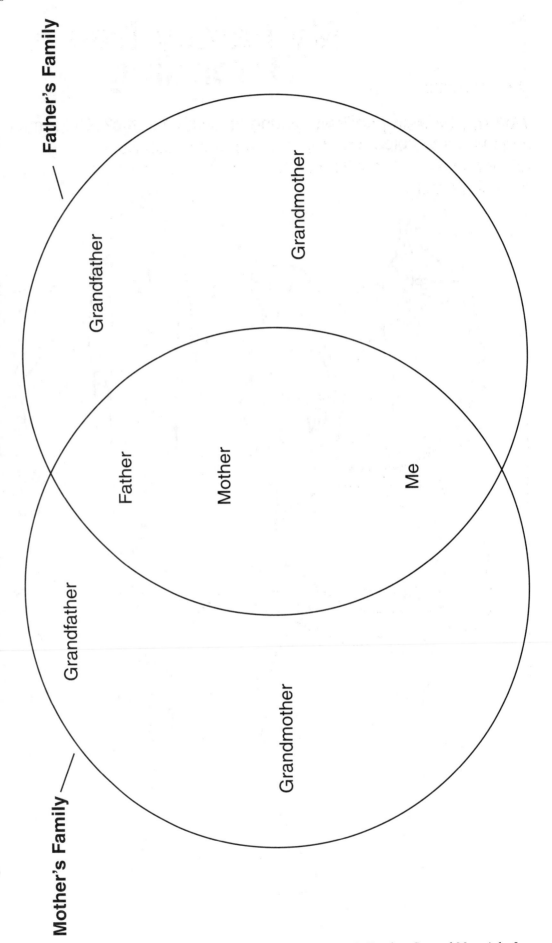

Father's Family

Grandfather

Grandmother

Father

Mother

Me

Mother's Family

Grandfather

Grandmother

My Family Tree

Dear Parents,

We are discussing families and how they grow. Please assist your child in completing this worksheet so that he or she can better understand family relationships. After writing in the names, have your child draw or paste pictures of each person.

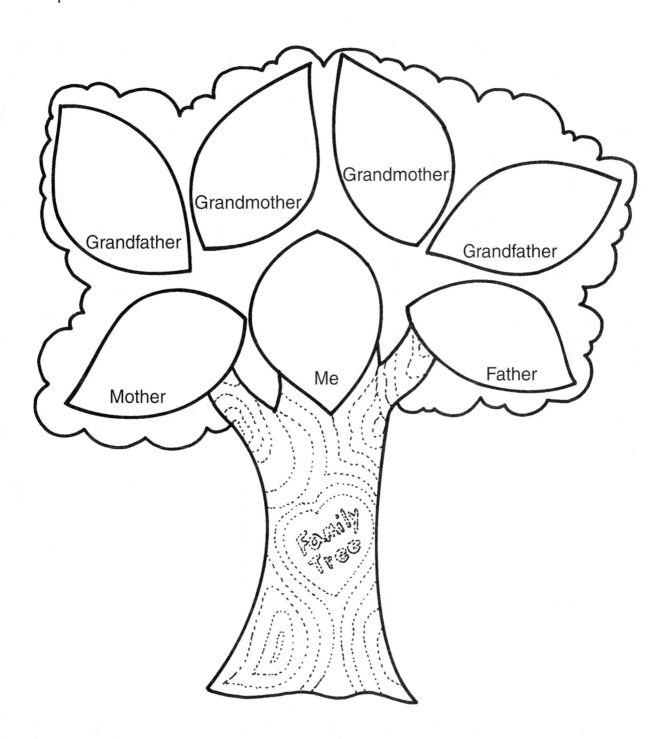

Poinsettia and Her Family

by Felicia Bond

Summary

Sometimes Poinsettia thinks her house is too small and her family is too big. She believes the house she lives in would be perfect without her noisy, messy, always-in-the-way brothers and sisters. However, when she is left all alone, she changes her mind.

The outline below is a suggested plan for using the various activities that are presented in this unit. You should adapt these ideas to fit your classroom situation.

Sample Plan

Day 1

- Do Setting the Stage activities 1 and 2, page 29.
- Read pages 1–16 of the book.
- Assign the house activity, page 34.
- Complete the Hidden Pigs activity, page 33.
- Assign a picture journal topic, page 41.
- Select a Music and Movement activity, pages 64–66.

Day 2

- Read pages 17–32 of the book.
- Assign the maze activity, page 36.
- Plant bean seeds, page 54.
- Match houses, page 52.
- Select a finger play, page 48.
- Assign a picture journal topic, page 41.
- Ask children to bring their favorite books.
- Send home recipe cards, page 70.

Day 3

- Match numbers and dots, page 35.
- Help the children count family members, page 56
- Create a new house, page 38.
- Select a Music and Movement activity, pages 64–66.
- Begin planning for the culminating activity, page 71.
- Make and send home pockets, page 32.

Day 4

- Discuss food groups, page 68.
- Discuss feelings. Assign page 39.
- Review the book by role playing, activity 3, page 30.
- Write a sequel to *Poinsettia and Her Family*, activity 7, page 30.
- Select a finger play, page 48.
- Make and send home invitations for the culminating activity.

Day 5

- Discuss other kinds of families, activity 9, page 31.
- Sequence the story, page 40.
- Match flowers and pigs, page 55.
- Make a mobile, page 62.
- Share favorite story books.
- Select a Music and Movement activity, pages 64–66.

Day 6

- Help the children create picture lockets, page 37.
- Complete same and different activities, pages 44 and 45.
- Make gingerbread families page 67.
- Practice finger plays, games, and music for party.
- Assign a picture journal topic, page 41.

Overview of Activities

Setting the Stage

1. Read the title of the book, *Poinsettia and Her Family*. Show the children the cover of the book. Then read the summary of the book to them. Ask the children about the sizes of their families. Do they like the size of their families? What do they think makes the best size family? Record what each child believes to be a perfect number for a family. Discuss the pros and cons of big families and small families. After hearing the discussion, ask the children if they would like to change the family size they recorded.

2. After looking at the cover of the book and reviewing the title, ask the children how this book may be different or similar to other books they have read about families. Explain that this is a story about talking animals and an example of one kind of fantasy. Ask them to name some other stories about animal families, like "The Three Little Pigs" and "Goldilocks."

Enjoying the Story

1. As you read the story, pause to explain vocabulary words, to elicit children's responses to the story, and to ask comprehension questions like the following:

- When does Poinsettia first begin to miss her family?
- How does Poinsettia's family happen to leave without her?
- If you were Poinsettia's mother, what would you say to her because she does not go along with the family?
- What do you think Poinsettia's family likes about their old house?
- What do you think Poinsettia learns about herself after being left alone? about her family?
- What do you think would have happened to Poinsettia if her family had not come back?
- Do you think Poinsettia and her family will be happy in their old house, now that they have returned? Explain.

2. Throughout the story Poinsettia experiences a range of feelings about her family. Have the children identify these feelings by completing page 39. Tell them to select one of the feelings and draw a picture about a time when they felt the same way.

3. Help the children familiarize themselves with Poinsettia's house by completing page 34.

4. Poinsettia had six brothers and sisters. Ask the children to match the pigs with the correct numerals on page 35. Continue the lesson by asking the children to complete the activity on page 55.

5. Tell the children to pretend that Poinsettia tries to find her family in their new home. Ask them to find their way through the maze on page 36 from the old house to the new house.

6. Poinsettia finds a picture of her family which she wears on a string around her neck. Help the children create their own picture lockets by completing the activity on page 37.

7. Different families live in different types and sizes of houses. Complete the house matching activity on page 52. If possible, take the children for a walk through a residential area. Before and during the walk, ask them to observe the houses. Are they the same, or are they different? What makes them different?

Overview of Activities *(cont.)*

Extending the Story

1. Say the words *Poinsettia* and *pig*, emphasizing the initial sound. Ask the children to identify the letter that makes the sound. Ask them to think of other words that begin with "P" and record the words on the chalkboard. Make copies of page 32 for each child. After the children color and cut out their pocket patterns, paste them to small manila envelopes. Send the pockets home with the children and ask them to draw or cut out pictures of things that begin with "P." Tell them to place their pictures in the pockets and to bring them back to school on a specified day. Allow children to display their pictures. This activity can easily be expanded by assigning other letter sounds.

2. Poinsettia came home from the library with her favorite book about a spotted circus horse who danced. Poinsettia had already read the book five times. Ask the children to bring in their favorite books—books they have read over and over. Then allow time for the children to share their books orally or display the books for children to browse through.

3. Role play the story of *Poinsettia and Her Family* by dividing the class into groups of four or five and assign children within the groups to take the roles of Poinsettia, her father, her mother, and one or two of her brothers and sisters. Ask them to role-play what they think Poinsettia and her family will do the next time she/they think the house is too small. Occasionally switch roles. Allow time to compare the roles played by each group.

4. To review the story, have the children complete the sequencing activity on page 40.

5. Read *The Perfect Family* by Nancy Carlson (Carolrhoda Books, Inc.) to the class. In this story Louanne, a pig, has a family of three, but she thinks a friend's family of ten is better. Compare Carlson's book with *Poinsettia and Her Family*.

6. Write the words *happy*, *sad*, *afraid*, and *angry* on the chalkboard. Discuss each of the words with the children and ask for examples of when they or Poinsettia may have had those feelings. Complete page 39.

7. Ask the children to assist you in writing a sequel to the story. Think about what might have happened if Poinsettia had moved with her family or if the family had not returned to find Poinsettia. Write the story on chart paper as the children dictate it. Assign small groups of students to illustrate each page. Display the completed pages on the bulletin board or create a clothesline with string or yarn and clip each page to it. Pages may also be bound as a Big Book for display in the library.

8. Give the children copies of page 38 and ask them to create a new house for Poinsettia's family by coloring the shapes, cutting them out, and pasting them to a piece of construction paper to form a house shape. If desired, have them add flowers, trees, etc.

Overview of Activities *(cont.)*

Extending the Story *(cont.)*

9. Prepare the word and picture cards as directed on pages 50 and 51. Tell the children that other groups can also be called families. Just as they are called "children," the younger members of animal families also have a group name. Give them one or more examples, like cat/kitten, dog/puppy. Ask the children to tell you other animal pairs that would be a family. List them on the chalkboard. Let the children take turns matching mothers and their babies. The cards may also be used to play a concentration game for one or two players. Turn all the cards face down on a table. The child turns over two of the cards. If they form a family group, he or she holds them. If they are not a group, the cards are returned to the table, facedown.

10. Food groups are also sometimes called families. Prepare the food chart from page 68. Ask the children to share their favorite foods and help them to classify them. To extend the activity, explain that everyone should eat five servings of fruits and vegetables a day. Have the children use fruit and vegetable stamps to make stickers, page 61. Give each child a copy of the record sheet on page 69. Ask the children to keep a record of the fruits and vegetables they eat for a week.

11. Families are rich with traditions and unique celebrations. Many celebrations feature special foods. Ask the children to name their favorite foods. Send copies of page 70 home to be completed by the child and his or her parent. Number the returned pages and make copies for each child. Make a "Family Favorites" cover and bind a set for each student. If desired, have the children assemble their own books. Pages may be stapled or punched and tied. Encourage parents to contribute samples of the recipes for snack time or for the culminating activity.

12. Poinsettia is fond of her mother's garden. Conduct the activities on page 54 to see how a plant grows.

13. Make gingerbread families, page 67, to serve at the culminating activity. If you prefer, use purchased sugar cookie dough. As an alternative, have the children create faces with icing and trims on plain, pre-baked cookies or cupcakes.

A Pocket of "P" Words

Directions: Discuss with the children that the word *Poinsettia* begins with the letter "P." Ask the children to think of other words that begin with "P" as you write them on the chalkboard. Then, for each child, duplicate the pocket below. Have the children color and cut out the pocket pattern and then glue it to a small manila envelope. Send the pockets home with the children and ask them to draw or cut out pictures that begin with "P." Tell them to place their pictures in the pocket and to bring it back to school on a specific day. Allow children to display their pictures.

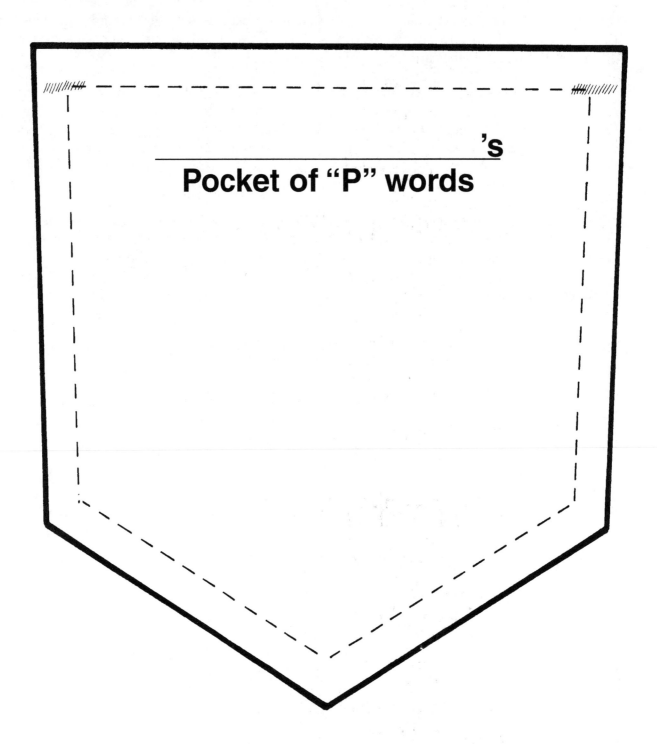

_____'s
Pocket of "P" words

Name _____

Hidden Pigs

Poinsettia's brothers and sisters are hiding in the garden. Can you find all of them? Color each one, and then count how many pigs there are.

Name _____

Following Directions

Directions: Follow the directions below to color Poinsettia's house and its surroundings.

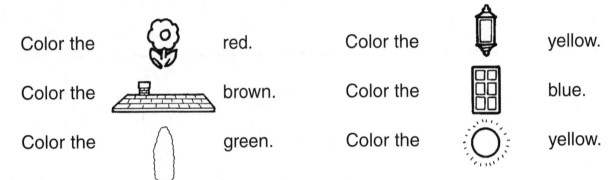

Color the   red.   Color the   yellow.

Color the   brown.   Color the   blue.

Color the   green.   Color the   yellow.

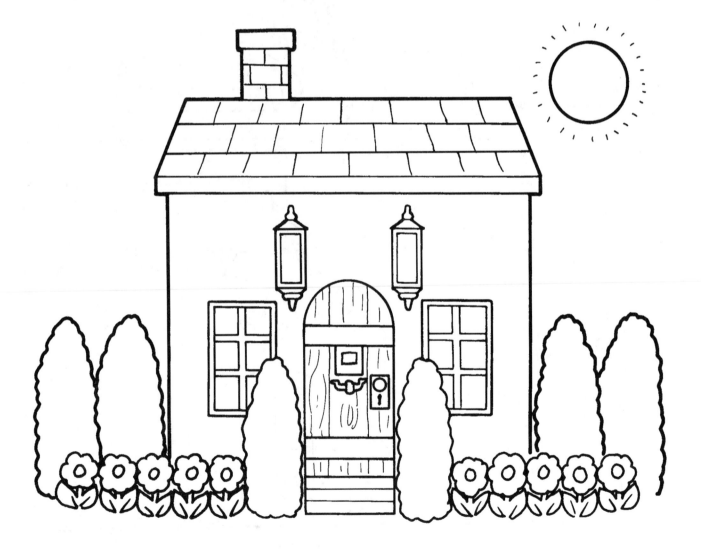

Name _____

Count the Dots

Directions: Count the dots on each of Poinsettia's brothers and sisters below and then draw a line to connect the pig with the correct numeral.

6

4

2

1

3

5

Find Your Way Home

Name _____

Directions: Draw a line from Poinsettia's old home to her new home. Do not cross any lines.

Poinsettia's old house

Poinsettia's new house

Picture Locket

Poinsettia found a picture of her family. She wore the picture on a string around her neck. Let each child make a picture locket of his or her family, using the frame below.

Materials:

yarn or string

macaroni or plastic drinking straws, cut in short lengths

large blunt yarn needles

tempera paint or food coloring (optional)

assorted beads, pasta shapes, cereal shapes, small buttons, etc.

hole punch

Directions:

- Make a copy of the pattern below on cardstock or poster board for each child. Punch two holes in the top of the frame.

- Ask each child to paste a photograph or draw a picture of his or her family on the solid piece.

- Create a frame by pasting pasta, cereal, buttons, etc., around the picture. Do not paste anything over the two holes at the top.

- Thread a piece of yarn or string through the holes and tie a knot.

- If desired, have the children thread cereal pieces, straw pieces, or macaroni shapes on their string or yarn before it is tied.

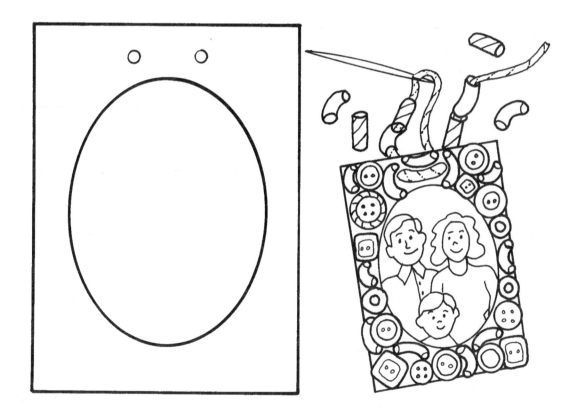

A New House

Directions: Color the shapes. Cut them out. Paste them on another piece of paper to make a new house for Poinsettia and her family.

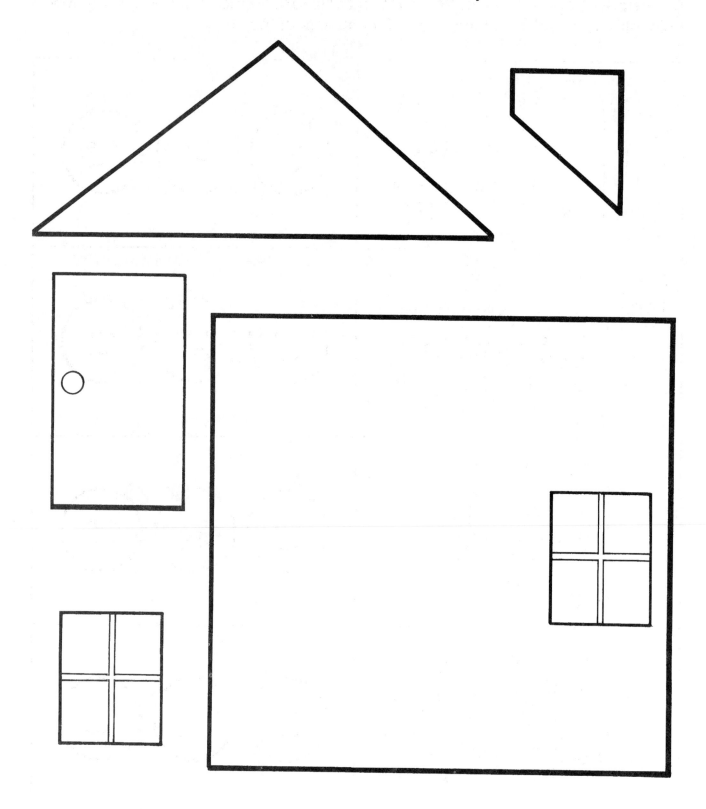

Name _____

Feelings

Directions: Look at the pictures. Draw a circle around the face that shows how Poinsettia was feeling during each of the events of the story.

Story Sequence

Directions: Color and cut out the pictures. Paste them in the right order on another piece of paper. In the empty square, draw what happens next.

40   © *Teacher Created Materials, Inc.*

Picture Journals

Picture Journals provide an opportunity for young children to respond to stories, concepts, and personal experiences, or to answer a general question posed by the teacher. Children should be encouraged to present stories in the proper sequence, and older or more advanced students may add words and/or simple sentences, referring to the posted word banks for spelling.

Make a book for each child, using construction paper for the covers and several sheeets of unlined paper. You may wish to use the pattern on page 15 to create a shape book. Older or more advanced children can assemble their own books. Demonstrate how to assemble the journal and ask students to decorate the cover.

Some questions and topics for journals are the following:

1. Ask the children to draw pictures of activities they like to do with their families.

2. Ask the children to think about the happy and sad times with their families and then illustrate these times.

3. Draw a picture that shows a family tradition.

4. Draw a favorite relative. Include something in the picture that shows what you do with this person.

5. Illustrate a scene from your family's favorite holiday.

6. Draw a picture of a place you like to visit with your family (zoo, amusement park, playground).

7. Draw a picture of the family pet.

8. What is your favorite place in your house? What do you do there?

9. Think about a place you have visited with your family. Draw a picture of it.

10. Draw a picture of someone in your family working.

Family Acrostics

Write the letters that make up the word *family* vertically on the chalkboard. Then ask the children to think of words that begin with each of these letters that would describe something about families. For example:

F—friendly, father
A—attentive, always there, aunt
M—mother
I—interested
L—loving
Y—you

Extend this activity by creating descriptions of family members: father, mother, sister, brother, etc.

Name _____

Family Words

Mother	⬭
Father	⬭
Sister	⬭
Brother	⬭

42

Name _____

Family Words *(cont.)*

Grandfather	⬭
Grandmother	⬭
Aunt	⬭
Uncle	⬭

Name _____

Word Families—Sounds Alike

Directions: Say the name of each picture. Draw a circle around the pictures that have the same sound as the first picture in each row.

| clock | block | lock | cat |
| hat | block | | |

cat	bat	hat	hen
cake	man	rake	hat
can	pan	bat	pig

Name _____

Word Families—Sounds Different

Directions: Say the name of each picture. Make an X over the word in each row that does not sound like the others.

can	man	fan	fish
coat	rock	goat	boat
cake	cat	hat	bat
pen	hen	ten	car
car	star	fish	jar

Which Does Not Belong?

Directions: Draw an X on the picture that does not belong to the group.

Name _____

Which Are the Same?

Directions: Color the pictures in each row that are the same.

Family Finger Plays

"Fine Family"
(Traditional)

Here is the family in my household.
Some are young,
And some are old.
Some are tall,
Some are small,
Some are growing just like me.
Together we all live as a family.
(Hold up one finger for each line, starting with the thumb.)

"Baby Grows"
(Traditional)

Five little fingers on this hand *(Hold up five fingers.)*
Five little fingers on that. *(Hold up five fingers on the other hand.)*
A dear little nose, *(Point to nose.)*
A mouth like a rose *(Point to mouth.)*
Two little cheeks so tiny and fat. *(Point to cheeks.)*
Two little eyes and two ears *(Point to eyes and then to ears.)*
And ten little toes, *(Point to toes.)*
That is the way the baby grows.

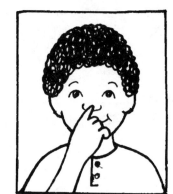

"Grandma's Spectacles"
(Traditional)

These are grandmother's spectacles, *(Make circles around eyes with fingers.)*
This is grandmother's hat. *(Use both hands and cup on head.)*
This is the way she folds her hands, *(Fold hands.)*
And puts them in her lap. *(Put hands in lap.)*

48

Name _____

Who Am I?

Directions: Draw a line through the word in each line that does not describe you. Draw a picture of yourself in the box.

I am

a son   a daughter.

I am

a sister   a brother.

I am

a grandson   a granddaughter.

I am

a nephew   a niece.

This is a
picture of
me.

Animal Mothers and Babies

Directions: Duplicate pages 50 and 51. Use markers, crayons, or colored pencils to color the pictures. Glue the pages to cardboard, laminate them, and then cut them apart. Place pictures of mother animals in one envelope and pictures of baby animals in another envelope. See activity 9 on page 31 for additional directions.

Dog	**Puppy**
Hen	**Chick**
Horse	**Colt**
Sheep	**Lamb**

50

Animal Mothers and Babies *(cont.)*

Cat	Kitten
Cow	Calf
Lion	Cub
Goose	Gosling

Name _____

Homes

Directions: Families live in many different kinds of homes. Draw a line between the homes that are alike.

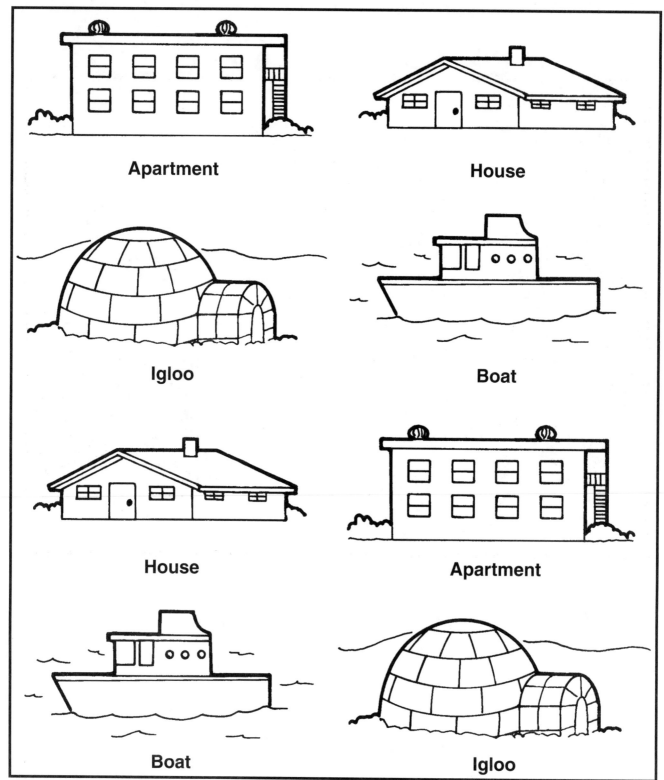

Apartment

House

Igloo

Boat

House

Apartment

Boat

Igloo

Name _____

My Family's Favorite Holiday

Directions: Families like to have parties. Color the picture. Add something to the picture that shows what kind of party it is and add yourself.

How many people are in the picture?_____

How many people are in your family?_____

Growing a Garden

Materials:

paper towels

clear resealable sandwich bags

masking tape

package of bean seeds

one Styrofoam cup for each child

potting soil

plastic or metal spoon

crayons or markers

Directions:

Soak the bean seeds overnight.

Fold a paper towel and place it in the sandwich bag. Dampen the towel and place five beans on it. Write your name on the bag. Close the bag, leaving a small opening for ventilation, and tape it to a warm sunny window.

Allow time each day for the children to observe the seeds. Discuss the changes that occur, and record them on a chart on the chalkboard. How many days does it take before the seeds sprout? When do they have leaves?

When the seedlings have produced leaves, it is time to transplant them. Cover the work surface with newspaper. Give each child a cup. Ask the children to write their names on the cups.

Use a pencil to poke a hole for drainage in the bottom of each cup.

Spoon soil into the cup. Carefully transfer the seedlings to the soil in the cup. Place the planted cups in a shallow pan or on a plate in a warm sunny place. Add 2 teaspoons (10 mL) water to each cup.

Allow time each day for the children to observe and water their beans.

Extensions

Provide an empty egg carton and several different types of bean seeds. Have the children sort the beans by size, color, etc. Discuss the similarities and differences. How many of each are there?

Name _____

Mrs. Pig's Garden

Directions: Draw a line from each group of pigs to the matching group of flowers.

Math

Name _____

How Many in My Family?

Directions: Have each child write the number of family members in the small box on the right. Ask the children to cut, color, and paste a set of that many hearts in the larger box.

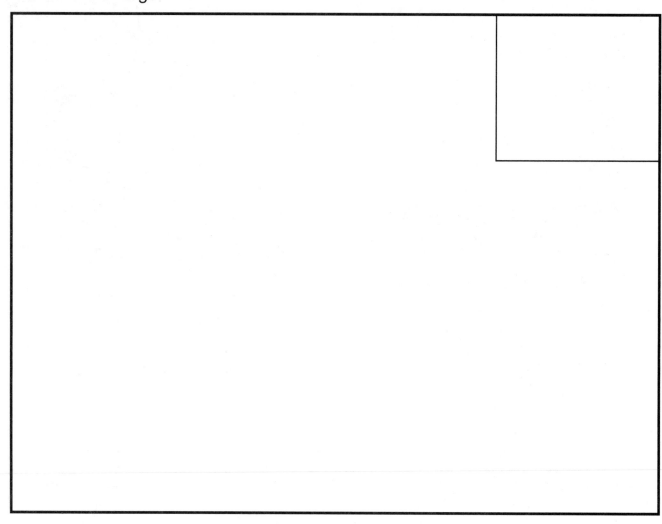

Family Charts and Graphs

To help the children understand how to organize information and to expand number concepts, use one or more of the following ideas:

1. Use double-sided tape or masking tape folded over on itself to make a large graph on a wall or chalkboard. As an alternative, attach parallel lines of yarn or string to the wall and provide spring-clip clothespins. (Lines may be vertical or horizontal.)

   To use the chart, decide on a question of the day and write it above the grid. Label the lines appropriately. Provide each child with a marker to use on the chart. Read the question out loud, and then call children one at a time to place their markers in the appropriate places on the chart. Discuss the results—which category has the most responses, which has the least, etc.

   Questions to ask:

   How many people are in your family?

   How many brothers do you have? How many sisters do you have?

   How many aunts do you have? How many uncles do you have?

   What is your family pet?

   What is your favorite fruit?

   What is your favorite vegetable?

   What is your favorite color?

2. If space permits, create a chart on the floor, using masking tape. To use this living graph, have the children stand in the space that represents their response. In addition to the questions above, ask questions that require the children to move from one category to another. Some examples are Do you have a big brother or a big sister? and Do you have a little brother or little sister?

Record the numbers on the chalkboard and discuss the fact that some people are in more than one category.

Family Puppets

Materials:

crayons and/or markers

scissors

glue

paper lunch sacks

copies of the circle pattern (pre-cut circles for younger children)

yarn (brown, black, yellow, red, gray, and white)

buttons, beads, fabric scraps, ribbon, etc. (optional)

Directions:

1. Give the children paper sacks and circles for each family member, including themselves.

2. Ask the children to draw in features and color a family member's face on each circle.

3. Assist them in cutting the circle in two just below the nose. Glue the top part of the face to the bottom of the bag, as shown. Glue the bottom part of the face under the flap, also as shown.

4. Let the children glue yarn hair to the top of each puppet's head. Have them color clothing on the bags. If desired, let them glue buttons, fabric scraps, etc., to the puppet's clothing.

5. Help the children write the family member's name and/or relationship on each bag puppet.

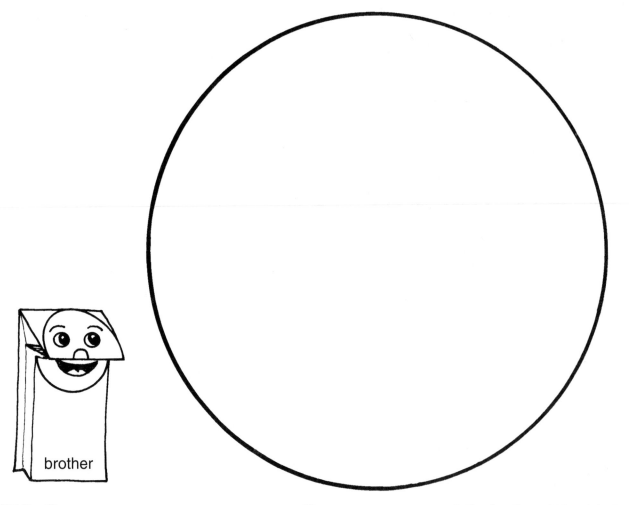

brother

Pop-up Family Portrait

Create a pop-up picture by following the directions below.

Materials: 2 pieces of 9" x 12" (24 x 30 cm) paper and one copy of page 60 for each child, glue, crayons, markers, or colored pencils

Directions: Have each child color and decorate a copy of the house on page 60. Next ask them to draw pictures of their families in the frame, or have them cut and paste pictures from magazines to represent their families.

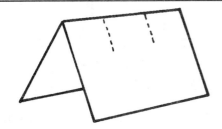

1. Fold one piece of paper in half widthwise. Cut a 1 ½" (3.75 cm) slit perpendicular to the fold 3" (8 cm) in from each side.

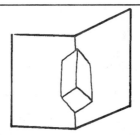

2. Open the fold, push the cut section through, and crease it to form the pop-up section.

3. Fold the second piece of paper in half and glue it to the first piece as shown to create a cover for the card.

4. Cut out the house picture and glue it to the cover.

5. Cut out the family picture and paste it to the pop-up section.

6. Assist the children in writing their family names on the insides of the cards.

Variations:

Change the text and the pictures to create an invitation for the culminating activity, page 71, or a greeting card.

Pop-up Family Portrait *(cont.)*

60

Family Stamp Pad Stickers

Materials:

rubber stamps in family themes

stamp pads in a variety of colors

fine-line markers (optional)

copies of the grid below

seal gum (see page 73)

Directions:

Have the children create stickers, using stamps and ink. If desired, have them use markers to add color. When they have filled the grid, place the page of stickers facedown and brush the seal gum on the back of the page (the paper may curl). Allow the page to dry thoroughly. When the page is dry, the children may cut the stickers apart and use them to decorate stationery, etc., by moistening the back.

Family Mobiles

Materials:

one wire coat hanger for each child

yarn or string

hole punch

one or more copies of the patterns below for each child

Directions:

Have the children color and cut out the patterns below, making one for each family.

Help them write their family member's names on the figures.

Punch a hole in the tab at the top of each picture.

Thread yarn or string through the holes and tie a knot in the end.

Tie each picture to the coat hanger.

Hang the completed mobiles around the classroom.

Family Puzzle

Directions: Find or draw a picture of something you like to do with your family. Paste it on the back side of the page. Turn the paper over and cut along the lines. Put the pieces back together again. Store your puzzle pieces in an envelope.

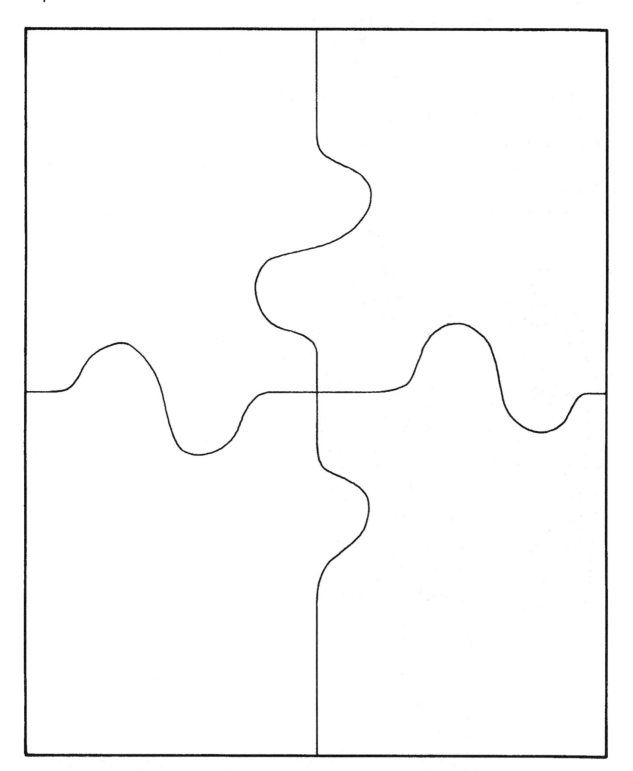

Music and Movement

Family Songs and Games

Many simple traditional songs feature family members. Others may be easily adapted to reinforce family concepts. Here are some to try:

1. Teach the children the following song (sung to the tune of "Here We Go 'Round the Mulberry Bush"):

> This is the way I help my family,
> Help my family, help my family.
> This is the way I help my family,
> All day long.
> This is the way I make my bed . . .
> This is the way I dress myself . . .
> This is the way I brush my teeth . . .

Ask the children to suggest other things they do to help their families. Change the fourth line accordingly to early in the morning, late in the afternoon, early in the evening, and so forth.

2. Teach the children another song about helping the family by singing and making up additional words to the following (sung to the tune of "Here We Are Together"):

> It's fun to be a helper, a helper, a helper.
> It's fun to be a helper, just anytime.
> Oh, I can wash the dishes, the dishes, the dishes.
> Oh, I can wash the dishes and make them shine.
> Oh, I can pick up the toys, the toys, the toys.
> Oh, I can pick up the toys and make the house tidy today.

Continue the song, using chores suggested by the children.

3. Use the tune of "The Farmer in the Dell" to teach the names of various family members and relatives. For example:

> The Farmer in the Dell,
> The Farmer in the Dell,
> Hi-ho the derry-o,
> The Farmer in the Dell.
>
> The Farmer takes a wife,
> The Farmer takes a wife,
> Hi-ho the derry-o,
> The Farmer takes a wife.
>
> The wife takes the child . . .
> The child takes a brother . . .
> The brother takes a sister . . .
> The sister takes a cousin . . .
> The cousin takes an aunt . . .
> The aunt takes an uncle . . .

64

Family Songs and Games *(cont.)*

Prior to beginning the game, write on the chalkboard the names of all relatives to be called. Others to add may include grandfather, grandmother, stepmother, stepfather, stepsister, stepbrother, etc.

To play this game have the children form a circle. Select one child to be the farmer and to get in the center of the circle. Then, the entire group sings the song as the farmer selects a wife. The wife goes into the center with the farmer. The game continues with children selected going into the center. After the last relative has been called to the center, the other children return to the circle as they sing:

The (name of relative) stands alone . . .

The last child called remains in the center and becomes the farmer for a new round of the song.

4. Teach the children the tune of "Brother John."

> Are you sleeping, are you sleeping,
> Brother John, Brother John?
> Morning bells are ringing, morning bells are ringing,
> Ding, ding, dong, ding, ding, dong.

Repeat, substituting new names and relationships like "sister Susie," "Uncle Tom," "Mommy dear," etc.

5. Help the children create verses about their relatives that they can sing to the tune of "Do You Know the Muffin Man?" Write their words on the chalkboard, and use the following as a pattern. For example:

> Do you know my cousin Tim,
> My cousin Tim, my cousin Tim?
> Oh, do you know my cousin Tim
> Who plays hide and seek with me?

I Packed My Suitcase

Ask the children to find or draw a picture of something that they would take with them when they go to visit relatives. Begin the chant with the whole group:

"I packed my suitcase to go to grandma's house, and in it I put . . ."

Call on one child to hold up his or her picture as he or she names the item. You may wish to have the child come to the front of the room.

Repeat the chant, adding the first child's item and calling on a second child.

"I packed my suitcase to go grandma's house, and in it I put a_____ and_____."

Continue until all the children have added to the suitcase.

Family Songs and Games *(cont.)*

Mommy Says, Daddy Says

Directions: Place a small stepstool or chair in an area where the children can move around easily. Then play a variation of "Simon Says." Use names of relatives—mommy, daddy, grandmother, aunt, cousin, etc.—instead of Simon's name.

Give children simple directions like "Mommy (or Daddy) says, walk around the chair." "Daddy says, sit down near the chair."

"Mommy says, go behind the chair." Continue with directions, using the following words: over, under, by, next to, on, beneath, up, around, etc.

The children should only follow those directions that include a relative's name. If the directions do not include a relative's name, the children should not follow the directions. Once the children are thoroughly familiar with how the game is played, let them take turns giving the directions.

Variations: Set up a maze that will allow the children to crawl under a table, step up and over a chair, walk around a stand, go between two chairs, etc. To make the game more challenging, you can combine two directions (for example, hop on one leg and crawl under the table, skip to the chair and then step up and over it.) Tell the children that if they successfully complete the maze, you will follow one of their mazes!

Over and Under

To reinforce the prepositional words, you can play the following game:

Cut a 12 inch (30 cm) circle from construction paper for each child, or give each child a paper plate. Have the children use their circles or plates as they follow simple one-step directions.

Put the circle *under* your foot.	Put the circle *below* your table.	Put the circle *between* your legs.
Put the circle *over* your head.	Put the circle *above* your chair.	Put the circle *under* your chin.

Mother, May I?

The children stand side by side on one side of the room, facing the teacher. The teacher acts out the role of "mother" or "father," naming a child and giving a direction, such as "Mary, take two baby steps forward." The named child responds with "Mother (or Father), may I?" The teacher then answers "Yes, you may." If the child forgets to ask for permission, he or she must remain in the same position. Play continues until one child reaches the teacher's position. He or she then becomes the mother or father, and the remaining children return to their starting position across the room. Vary the directions for each child by changing the kind of movement and/or the number of moves.

Some directions to try:

- Take (number) baby steps.
- Take (number) giant steps.
- Take (number) hops.

- Take (number) jumps.
- Skip (number) times.

As the children become more proficient, combine two or more directions. For older children, you may vary the script as follows:

"Mary, take two baby steps forward."
"Mother, may I?"
"No, you may not. Take three hops forward."
"Mother, may I?"
"Yes, you may."

Gingerbread Family

Gingerbread Dough

Ingredients:

$^1/_2$ cup (125 mL) shortening

$^1/_2$ cup (125 mL) sugar

$^1/_2$ cup (125 mL) dark molasses

$^1/_4$ cup (65 mL) water

2 $^1/_2$ cups (625 mL) flour

(Omit salt and baking soda if using self-rising flour.)

$^3/_4$ teaspoon (3.75 mL) salt

$^1/_2$ teaspoon (2.5 mL) baking soda

$^3/_4$ teaspoon (3.75 mL) ground ginger

$^1/_4$ teaspoon (1.25 mL) nutmeg

$^1/_8$ teaspoon (0.6 mL) allspice

icing (see below) or tubes of decorator's icing in assorted colors

raisins, small candies, etc., for decorating

Directions:

1. Cream the shortening and sugar together in a bowl. Stir in the molasses, water, flour, salt, baking soda, ginger, nutmeg, and allspice. Cover with plastic wrap and chill for 2 to 3 hours.

2. Roll the dough on a lightly floured board into a sheet about $^1/_4$ inch (.65 cm) thick.

3. Provide different sizes of gingerbread cookie cutters for children to use, and allow them to cut out members of their families. Place the cut cookies on ungreased cookie sheets and bake at 375° F (190° C) for 10 to 12 minutes. Cool on a wire rack.

Icing (makes 3 cups/750 mL)

Ingredients:

8 cups (2 L) confectioners' sugar

4 tablespoons (60 mL) water, plus additional

variety of food colors

Preparation:

1. Mix the sugar and water in a bowl. Add more water, 1 teaspoon (5 mL) at a time, until the icing can be easily spread but holds its shape. Divide the icing into several bowls. Add a few drops of food coloring to each to create different colors.

2. Ice the cookies, using plastic knives. To make disposable decorating tubes, spoon icing into sandwich-size plastic bags. Cut off a small piece from one corner of the bag.

3. Add raisins, candies, etc., if desired.

Food Families

Copy the pyramid at the bottom of this page on the chalkboard, or make a large copy for the bulletin board. Discuss the five food groups with the children as you point out the pictures that belong to each group. Ask each child to name a favorite food, and help the child decide which food group best represents his or her choice. Write the child's name in the appropriate category.

Discuss the "five a day for healthful eating." Have the children make fruit and vegetable stickers (see page 61). Make copies of page 69 for each child. Provide time for the children to chart their healthful eating for a week.

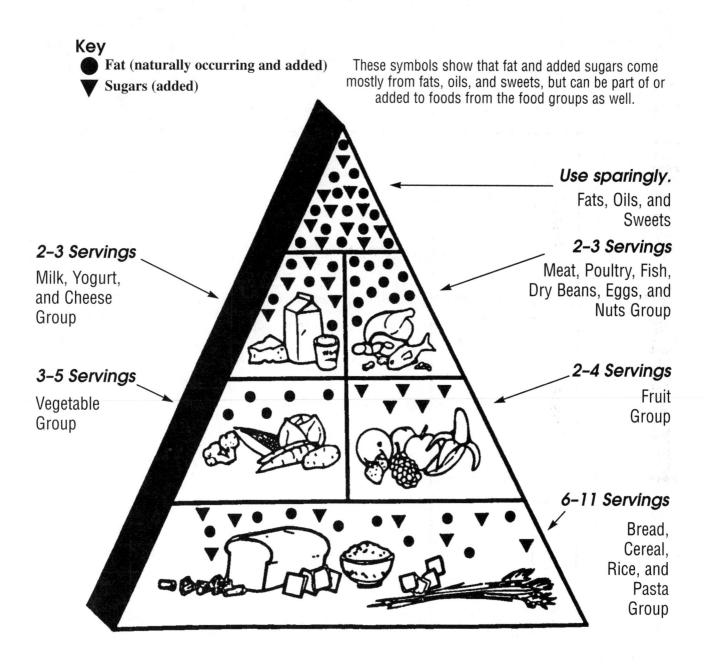

Key
● **Fat (naturally occurring and added)**
▼ **Sugars (added)**

These symbols show that fat and added sugars come mostly from fats, oils, and sweets, but can be part of or added to foods from the food groups as well.

Use sparingly.
Fats, Oils, and Sweets

2–3 Servings
Meat, Poultry, Fish, Dry Beans, Eggs, and Nuts Group

2–3 Servings
Milk, Yogurt, and Cheese Group

3–5 Servings
Vegetable Group

2–4 Servings
Fruit Group

6–11 Servings
Bread, Cereal, Rice, and Pasta Group

Five-a-Day Healthful Eating

Name _____

Monday	Tuesday	Wednesday	Thursday	Friday

Life Skills

My Family's Favorite Foods

Dear Parents,

As part of our unit on families, we are discussing food groups and favorite foods. Please help your child select a favorite food and complete the attached recipe card. Share as much information as possible about the recipe with your child. Where did it originate? Is it part of a special celebration? Ask your child to illustrate the recipe card on the back.

All of the recipes will be duplicated and included in our Family Favorites Cookbook. If you would like to share a sample of the recipe with the class, please contact me.

Sincerely,

_____
Teacher

[Recipe card with blank lines for writing]

Family Fun Fair

To end the unit and synthesize learning, help the children plan a Fun Fair to celebrate families.

1. Talk about the things that families do to prepare for special gatherings. Involve the children in planning for decorations, a program, refreshments, and inviting guests.

2. Create a family show-and-tell time by sending home the note at the bottom of this page, explaining family show-and-tell and asking each family to bring as many family members to school as they can. Point out that it is very interesting and educational to have families share their cultures and family traditions.

3. Have the children make invitations, following the pop-up picture directions on page 59. Print or type the invitation and make a copy for each child. As an alternative, write the invitation on the chalkboard, and have older or more advanced children copy it on the stationery (page 78).

4. Have the children help in preparing displays of their family projects.

5. Practice one or more of the Family Finger Plays (page 48) and/or songs (pages 64 and 65) to present to the families.

6. Help the children prepare simple refreshments like fruits and vegetables or sandwiches. You may ask parents to bring their children's favorite snacks or desserts to share with the class.

7. Allow time for each child to introduce his or her family to the class.

Letter to Parents

Dear Parent,

We have been learning all about families. Now we would like to meet as many of your family members as possible. We would like you and/or representatives of your family to come to school between
_____and_____on_____to
see what we have learned. Please bring something to share that is special to your family. You can share a favorite family food, a song, photographs, a special holiday, a game, a pet . . . be creative! We just want to get to know your family.

Please feel free to bring as many family members as you can. We look forward to seeing you.

Sincerely,

_____
Teacher

Activity Centers to Encourage Family Concepts

Create one or more activity centers in the classroom. These may be used for free play or as assigned for independent or small group tasks.

1. Create a "home-living" center by providing play props to represent a home, such as a play kitchen area with a stove, sink, refrigerator, table, chairs, pots, pans, dishes, pretend foods, and so forth. Also, provide dress-up clothes for both male and female roles.

2. Provide a dollhouse with moveable furniture and multi-ethnic family figures.

3. Create a block-building center that includes street signs, multi-ethnic family figures, cars, vans, and trucks. Encourage the children to build houses and apartment buildings and to create their own neighborhoods.

4. Set up a puppet stage and provide various multi-ethnic family figures. Stick puppets could be made by duplicating the family figures on pages 76 and 77 and gluing them to tongue depressors. Paper bags, yarn, construction paper, and other materials can be provided for children to make their own "family" puppets. Encourage the children to create plays or skits about their families.

5. Create an art center by providing clay, construction paper, magic markers, magazines, catalogs, and other assorted art materials. Ask the children to create something that represents their families. For example, they can make clay figures to represent their families, create a collage by cutting and pasting pictures from magazines or catalogs, and so forth.

6. Create a writing center in which you supply paper, pencils, markers, staplers, and/or preconstructed blank books. Encourage the children to create illustrations and to write stories about their families. Allow time to share.

7. Set up a family picture center in which pictures are displayed showing different family lifestyles and showing as many ethnic groups as possible. Make a space available for children to display family photos or drawings that they wish to share.

8. Create a families-at-work center in which you provide as many figures as possible to represent various jobs—doctor, nurse, barber, firefighter, pilot, waitress, chef, grocer, carpenter, etc. Provide dress-up clothes and props that represent different jobs. Allow time for children to explore and dramatize.

9. Create a center that has a variety of boxes—cereal, shoe, tissue, milk carton, etc., plus paint, paper, tape, markers, glue, and so on. Ask the children to create their own houses. If space is available, set up a miniature village of box houses.

10. Provide wooden clothespins, markers, scraps of yarn, cloth, and construction paper. Ask the children to create the members of their families by creating clothespin people. Allow time for the children to share their "clothespin family."

11. Provide sets of family flannelboard characters and a flannelboard. Allow time for children to use flannelboard characters to introduce their families.

Craft Recipes

These may be prepared by the teacher in advance or done as a class project to reinforce measurement and following directions.

Cornstarch Clay

2 cups (500 mL) cornstarch

1 ¹/₂ cups (375 mL) salt

1 cup (250 mL) water

4 colors of food coloring

Have the children help to measure the cornstarch, salt, and water, allowing them to touch each ingredient and describe it. Mix them together in a pan. An adult needs to cook these ingredients over a medium heat, stirring constantly, until the mixture boils and thickens to a gel-like consistency (approximately 15 minutes). Divide the mixture into four small bowls. Discuss with the children how the ingredients are the same/different before and after cooking. Add one color of food coloring to each container and mix. When cool, allow the children to use the clay to create shapes of different family members. You may want to encourage children to mix two colors of clay together to create new colors.

Clay

2 cups (500 mL) flour

¹/₂ cup (125 mL) salt

¹/₂ tablespoon (7.5 mL) vegetable oil

powdered paint of desired color

Mix flour, salt, and powdered paint together. Add oil. Knead in enough water to make a thick dough. Store in an airtight container. Clay can be left in the air to dry or be baked in a 300° F (150° C) oven until hard.

Use the recipe above to make handprint plaques. Put approximately ³/₄ inch (1.8 cm) of clay in a tinfoil pie plate large enough to fit a child's hand. Press the child's hand into the clay to make an imprint and then remove the hand. Use a pencil to inscribe the child's name and date. Allow the print to dry for several days. Remove the plaque from the pan.

Seal Gum

1 ¹/₄ oz (35 g) envelope unflavored gelatin

1 tablespoon (15 mL) cold water

3 tablespoons (45 mL) boiling water

¹/₂ teaspoon (2.5 mL) white corn syrup

¹/₂ teaspoon (2.5 mL) lemon extract

baby food jar

Pour gelatin onto cold water and allow to soften for 5 minutes. Add boiling water, stirring until the gelatin dissolves. Add corn syrup and flavoring. (Store any unused gum in a sealed jar in the refrigerator. Place the jar in a pan of hot water to soften it before the next use.) **Note:** The syrup and flavoring are optional. You may use sugar, a different flavor, or omit one or both items.

Family Bulletin Boards

1. *This Is Me, and I'm Part of My Family*

   Several days prior to creating the "This Is Me" bulletin board, send a note home to parents, asking for a family photo and a recent photo of their child. Be sure to communicate with the parents that they should not send valuable, one-of-a-kind photos. Place the caption "This Is Me, and I'm Part of My Family" on the bulletin board in large letters. When all photos have been collected, arrange the children's pictures on the bulletin board, allowing space to place the family photos and their names next to their photos. Display the family photos across the bottom of the bulletin board or on a nearby table. Gather the children around the bulletin board and ask them to match each family photo to the child's photo that goes with it. Then place the child's name and family photo next to the child's photo.

   Variations: If a camera is available, take photos of the children at school.

   Instead of family photos, ask the children to draw pictures of their families, or have them cut pictures from magazines to represent their families.

2. *A Family Is . . .*

   Cover a bulletin board with light-colored paper and write the caption "A Family Is . . ." on it. Read the caption to the children and ask them to think of words or phrases that describe what a family is. Write the words and phrases around the edge of the bulletin board. Provide magazines and ask the children to cut out pictures of families that would help to illustrate the words and phrases written on the bulletin board, or ask the children to draw pictures for the board. Attach the pictures to the bulletin board and ask the children for any additional words and phrases.

3. *Families at Work*

   Create a "Families at Work" bulletin board in which you and the children find pictures of various jobs held by parents of the children. Then put a photo or name of each child by a picture of his or her parent's type of work. Be sure to include pictures that reflect other tasks, such as caring for family, cleaning house, etc. Encourage children to add pictures showing things that they do to help their families.

   Variation: Use the theme "Families at Play." Ask the children to find or draw pictures of favorite family activities.

4. *Our Classroom Family*

   Give each child a paper plate. Provide yarn, string, crayons and/or markers, buttons, etc. Ask each child to create a self-portrait, using the plate and adding details. Mount and label.

Parent Letter

Dear Parents,

We are beginning a thematic unit on families. We will be reading several books about families and doing a variety of family-oriented activities. To make this unit more meaningful, I would appreciate your help. As this unit progresses, you will be asked to help your child complete some of the activities that call for family information. Please share as much as you can with your child.

We will also need photographs for several art projects. If possible, please send a current picture of your child and one or more snapshots of your family. Send copies if possible, as these will not be returned.

To enrich your child's learning experience, please do some or all of the following activities:

- Share family photo albums and videos with your child, identifying family members. Discuss your family history.

- Tell your child stories about your family when you were young.

- Help your child write letters to send to members of your extended family.

- Take your child to the library. Help him or her select a family storybook, poetry book, or nonfiction book. Read it together and discuss your favorite parts.

- Together, watch a children's movie that has a positive family at its center, like *The Swiss Family Robinson* (Walt Disney Home Video, 1992) or *The Sound of Music* (Argyle Entertainment, Inc./Twentieth Century Fox, 1965). Discuss the movie and the family it portrays with your child.

- Celebrate your family by preparing a special meal that includes favorite family foods. Let your child assist in preparing the food, setting the table, etc. Talk about the origins of the various dishes—Aunt Sally's beans, Grandma's biscuits, etc.

Sincerely,

_____
Teacher

Family Figure Patterns

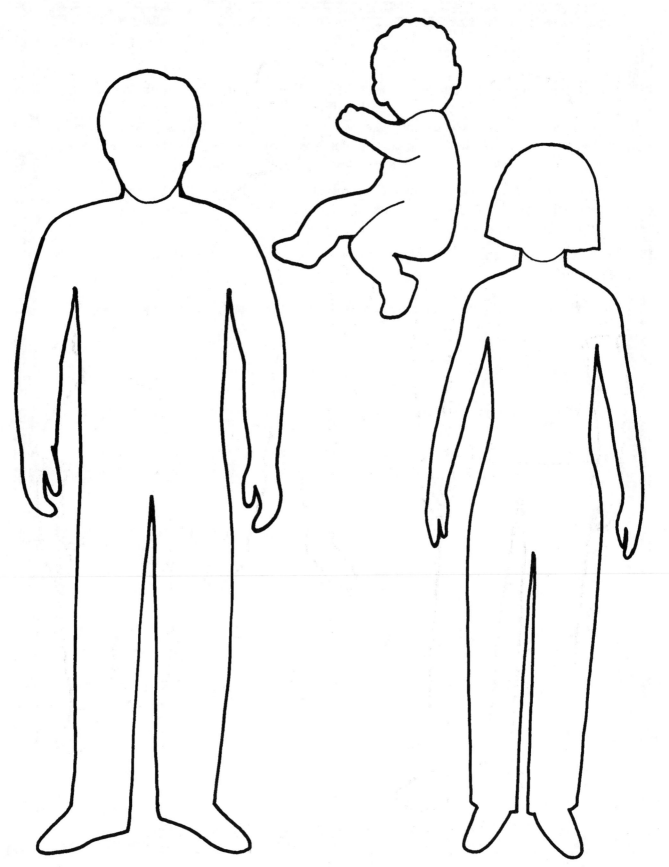

Family Figure Patterns *(cont.)*

Stationery

Awards

Achievement Award

_____

has earned our Classroom Family Award

for _____

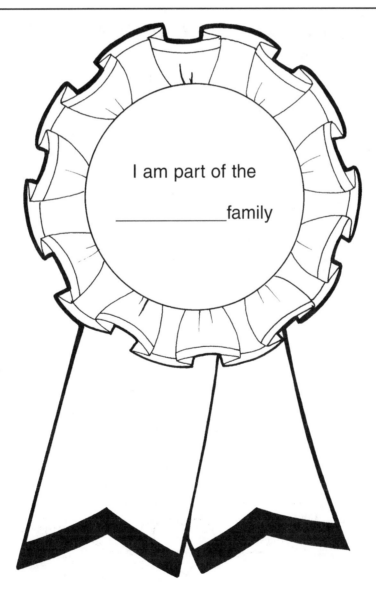

I am part of the

_____ family

Bibliography

Alexander, Martha. *Nobody Asked Me If I Wanted a Baby Sister*. Dial Books, 1987

Aliki. *The Two of Them*. Morrow, 1987

Berry, Jay. *Teach Me About Brothers and Sisters*. Children's Press, 1987

Berry, Jay. *Teach Me About Mommies and Daddies*. Children's Press, 1987

Berry, Jay. *Teach Me About Relatives*. Children's Press, 1987

Blume, Judy. *The One in the Middle Is the Green Kangaroo*. Bradbury Press, 1981

Boegehold, Betty. *Daddy Doesn't Live Here Anymore*. Western, 1985

Bonners, Susan. *The Wooden Doll*. Lothrop, Lee, and Shepard, 1991

Brimmer, Larry Dane. *Elliot Fry's Good-Bye*. Boyds Mill Press, 1994

Brown, Margaret Wise. *The Runaway Bunny*. Harper & Row, 1942

Caines, Jeanette. *Daddy*. Harper & Row, 1977

Carle, Eric. *My Apron*. Philomel Books, 1994

Carlson, Nancy. *Louanne Pig in the Perfect Family*. Carolrhoda Books, Inc., 1986

Christiansen, C. B. *My Mother's House, My Father's House*. Atheneum, 1989

Cooke, Trish. *So Much*. Candlewick, 1994

Crews, Donald. *Bigmama's*. Greenwillow Books, 1991

Drescher, Joan. *Birth-Order Blues*. Viking, 1993

Drescher, Joan. *My Mother's Getting Married*. Dial Books for Young Readers, 1986

Flournoy, Valerie. *Tanya's Reunion*. Dial Books, 1995

Girard, Linda. W. *At Daddy's on Saturdays*. Albert Whitman, 1987

Goldman, Susan. *Cousins Are Special*. Alert Whitman & Co., 1978

Hall, Donald. *The Ox-cart Man*. Viking Press, 1979

Hausherr, Rosmarie. *Celebrating Families*. Scholastic, 1997

Helmering, Doris Wild. *I Have Two Families*. Abingdon, 1981

Hoban, Russell. *A Baby Sister for Frances*. Harper & Row Publishers, 1964

Hoberman, Mary Ann. *Fathers, Mothers, Sisters, Brothers*. Puffin Books, 1991

Hoffman, Mary. *Amazing Grace*. Dial, 1991

Hoffman, Mary. *Boundless Grace*. Dial, 1995

Johnston, Tony. *The Quilt Story*. G. P. Putnam's, 1985

Johnston, Tony. *The Iguana Brothers*. Blue Sky Press/Scholastic, 1995

Jones, Rebecca C. *Great Aunt Martha*. Dutton, 1995

Joosse, Barbara. *Mama, Do You Love Me?* Dial, 1991

Kalman, Bobbie. *People in My Family*. Crabtree, 1985

Keats, Ezra Jack. *Peter's Chair*. Harper & Row, 1967

Kroll, Virginia. *Beginnings: How Families Came to Be*. Albert Whitman Co. 1996

Lasker, Joe. *He's My Brother*. Albert Whitman, 1974

Leedy, Loreen. *Who's Who in My Family?* Holiday House, 1995

McMillan, Bruce. *Grandfather's Trolley*. Candlewick Press, 1995

Merriam, Eve. *Daddies at Work*. Simon & Schuster, 1989

Ormerod, Jan. *101 Things to Do with a Baby*. Lothrop, Lee, & Shepard Books, 1984

Polacco, Patricia. *Thunder Cake*. Scholastic, 1990

Rogers, Paul and Emma. *Our House*. Candlewick, 1993

Rotner, Shelley and Sheila McKelly. *Lots of Moms!* Dial, 1996

Schick, Eleanor. *City in the Winter*. Collier Books, 1970

Senisi, Ellen B. *Brothers & Sisters*. Scholastic, 1993

Seuling, Barbara. *What Kind of Family Is This?* Western, 1985

Sharmat, Marjorie. *Sometimes Mama and Papa Fight*. Harper & Row, 1980

Sharratt, Nick. *Snazzy Aunties*. Candlewick Press, 1994

Skutch, Robert. *Who's in a Family?* Tricycle Press, 1995

Steel, Danielle. *Martha's New Daddy*. Delacorte Press, 1989

Steptoe, John. *Stevie*. Harper & Row, 1969

Waddell, Martin. *Once There Were Giants*. Candlewick Press, 1995

Ward, Sally G. *Charlie and Grandma*. Scholastic, 1986

Ward, Sally G. *Molly and Grandpa*. Scholastic, 1986

Watson, J. Werner, R. E. Switzer, and J. C. Hirschberg. *Sometimes a Family Has to Split Up*. Crown, 1988

Watson, Mary. *The Butterfly Seeds*. Tambourine Books, 1995

Whelan, Gloria. *Bringing the Farmhouse Home*. Simon & Schuster, 1992